Hello Ricott, I'm princess Nathashi

____

____

Authored & Designed by Kanishka EdiriSinghe

Published by Kanishka EdiriSinghe

First Edition: 2024

ISBN-13: 979-8884375062

For permissions requests, write to the publisher at —
kanishka.edirisinghe@outlook.com

Printed in the USA

Ricott the Gecko

"My Dear Ricott,
You were the best part of my childhood. Your small paws and cute eyes always brought happiness to my life. You were more than just a pet to me, you were a true friend who was always there to listen, comfort, and play.
I'm grateful to my loving parents who taught me the importance of taking care of someone else and brought us together. You taught me about loyalty and the true meaning of friendship. The memories we shared will always be special to me."
"With love,"

Kanishka EdiriSinghe.

by Kanishka EdiriSinghe

Once in a while,
in the Ricott's
magical garden,

A truly
enchanting
incident
unfolded.

From a faraway
Kingdom, a princess
named 'Nathashi' came
through a magical
portal in search of
adventure and new
friends.

Suddenly Ricott and Princess Nathashi met each other.

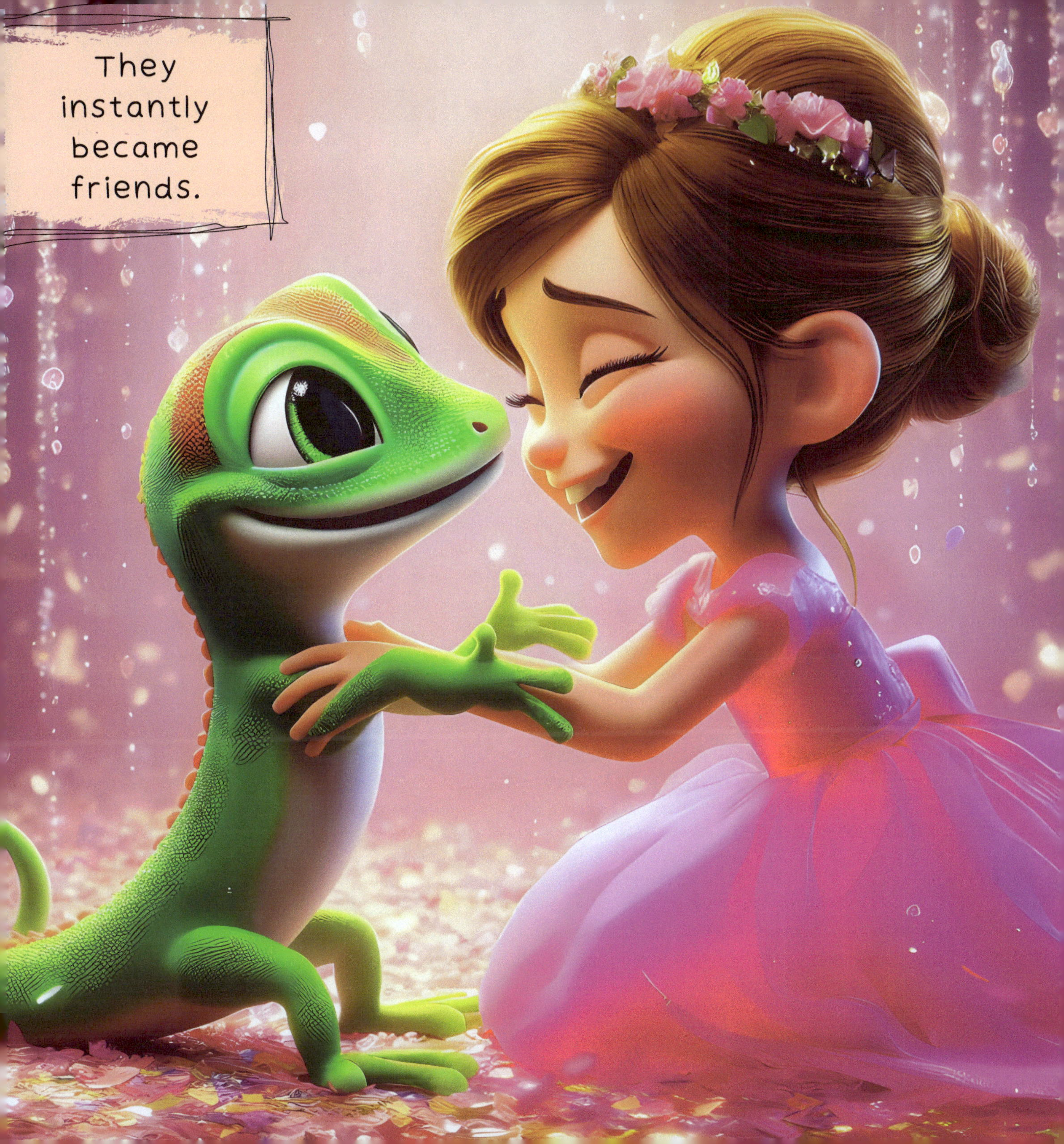
They
instantly
became
friends.

Ricott invited
her to join him
in an exciting
venture.

After that,
they decided
to organize a
royal picnic.

They invited all their friends to the magical garden.
See you soon, picnic spoon!

Ricott went on an incredible quest with the princess to collect candies and decorations for their royal picnic.

When they entered the garden's hidden corners, they discovered a variety of candies including Smarties, Reese's Cups, Snickers, and Sour Patch Kids.

As the day
wore on, the
garden turned
into a colorful
paradise.

The garden became
a bright wonderland
with shimmering
lights and delicate
blossoms.

As the day went on
Ricott and the
princess, convened
with their friends for
the grand picnic
under the warm sun.

They crafted splendid memories that rippled throughout the magical garden.

They enjoyed delicious snacks such as chocolates, chips, crackers, and pretzels and shared their stories.

The atmosphere
was filled with
joy, unity, and
the spirit of
friendship.

Eventually, Ricott and Princess Nathashi became best friends. They held each other tight, wrapped arms around, and nestled lovingly.

Lessons learned about group work, friendship, and the impact of working together resonated in the hearts of all the creatures in the garden.

At the end of
the day, the
princess
gracefully took
her leave.

Far Away Kingdom
She promised to return soon with a well-Kept hidden secret.

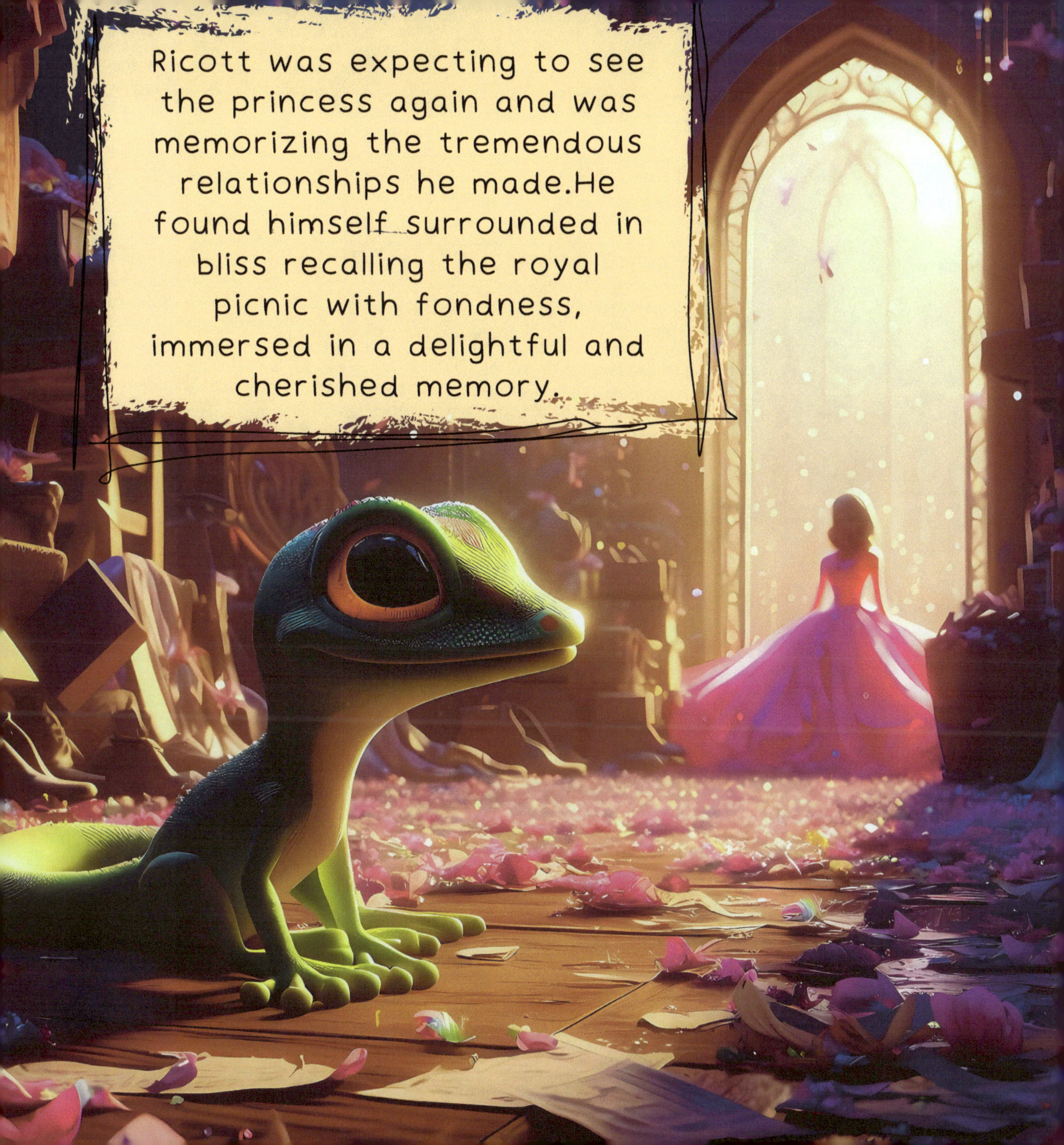

Ricott was expecting to see the princess again and was memorizing the tremendous relationships he made.He found himself surrounded in bliss recalling the royal picnic with fondness, immersed in a delightful and cherished memory.

As the night began its gentle embrace, Ricott fell into a deep slumber feeling reposed and thrilled, impatient to explore more of the garden tomorrow.

THE END... FOR NOW

Dear little one,

Give me a high five, kiddo! My name is Uncle Kanishka. As I write this letter, my heart is filled with so much love and joy for you. When I was around your age, I had a pet Gecko named Ricott, and he was my best friend. It was so much fun to imagine all kinds of adventures with him, just like you're doing now with this story.

I'm assuming that your mom or dad is reading this letter to you, right? Hi there, parents! I hope you're enjoying the story as much as your little one is. And speaking of little ones, kiddo, I can't wait for you to grow up and look back at these books as cherished memories of our time together.

Remember, kiddo, that I'm always here for you. Whenever you need someone to talk to, to share your dreams and fears, or just a friendly ear to listen to, you can always reach out to me. Just send me an email. I'm here to support and cheer you on in everything you do.

Always be a good kid to your parents and know that they love you more than anything in the world. You have a bright future ahead of you, and I can't wait to see all the wonderful things you'll accomplish.

Sending you all my love and best wishes,

Uncle Kanishka EdiriSinghe.

kanishka.edirisinghe@outlook.com

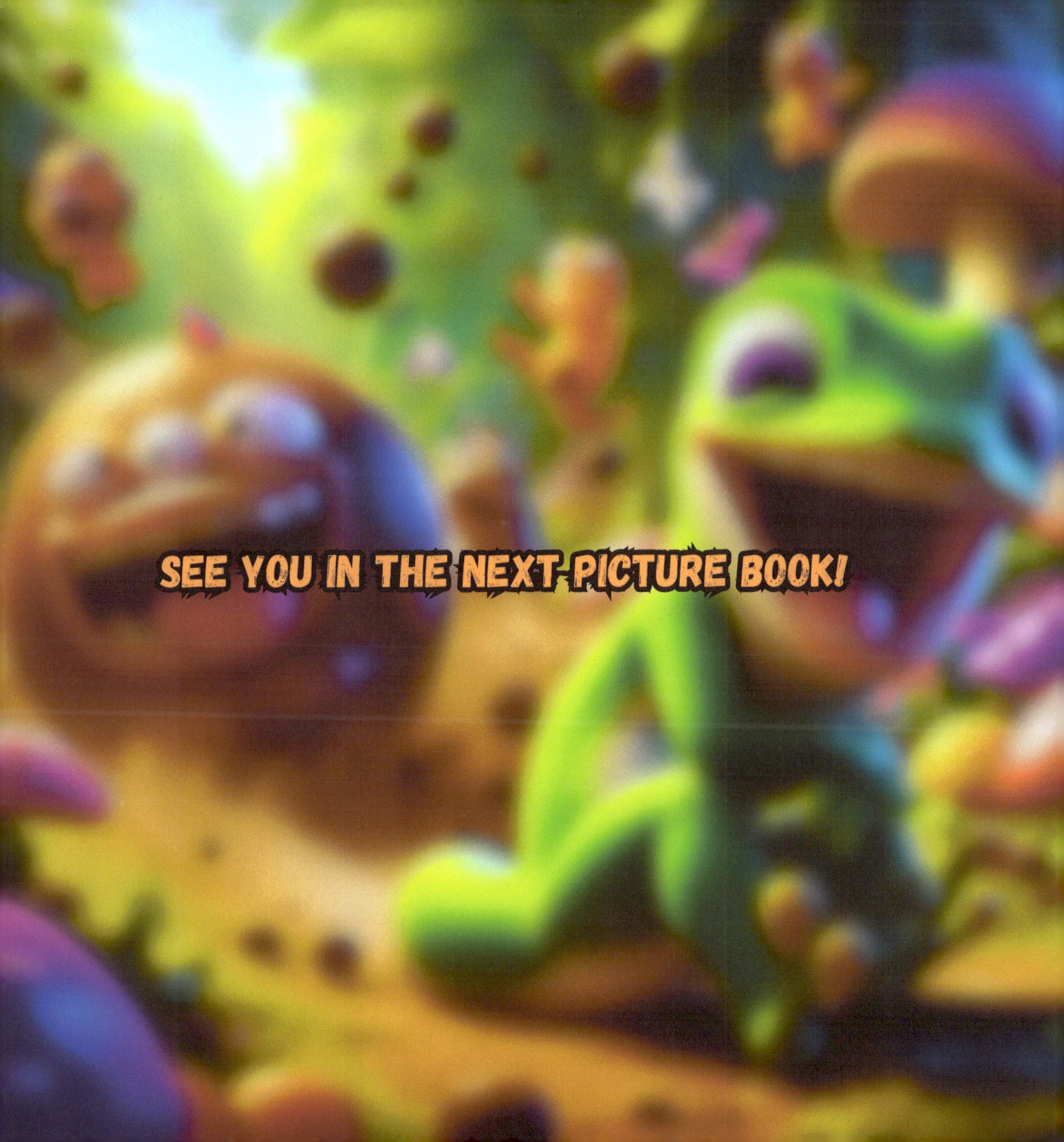
SEE YOU IN THE NEXT PICTURE BOOK!

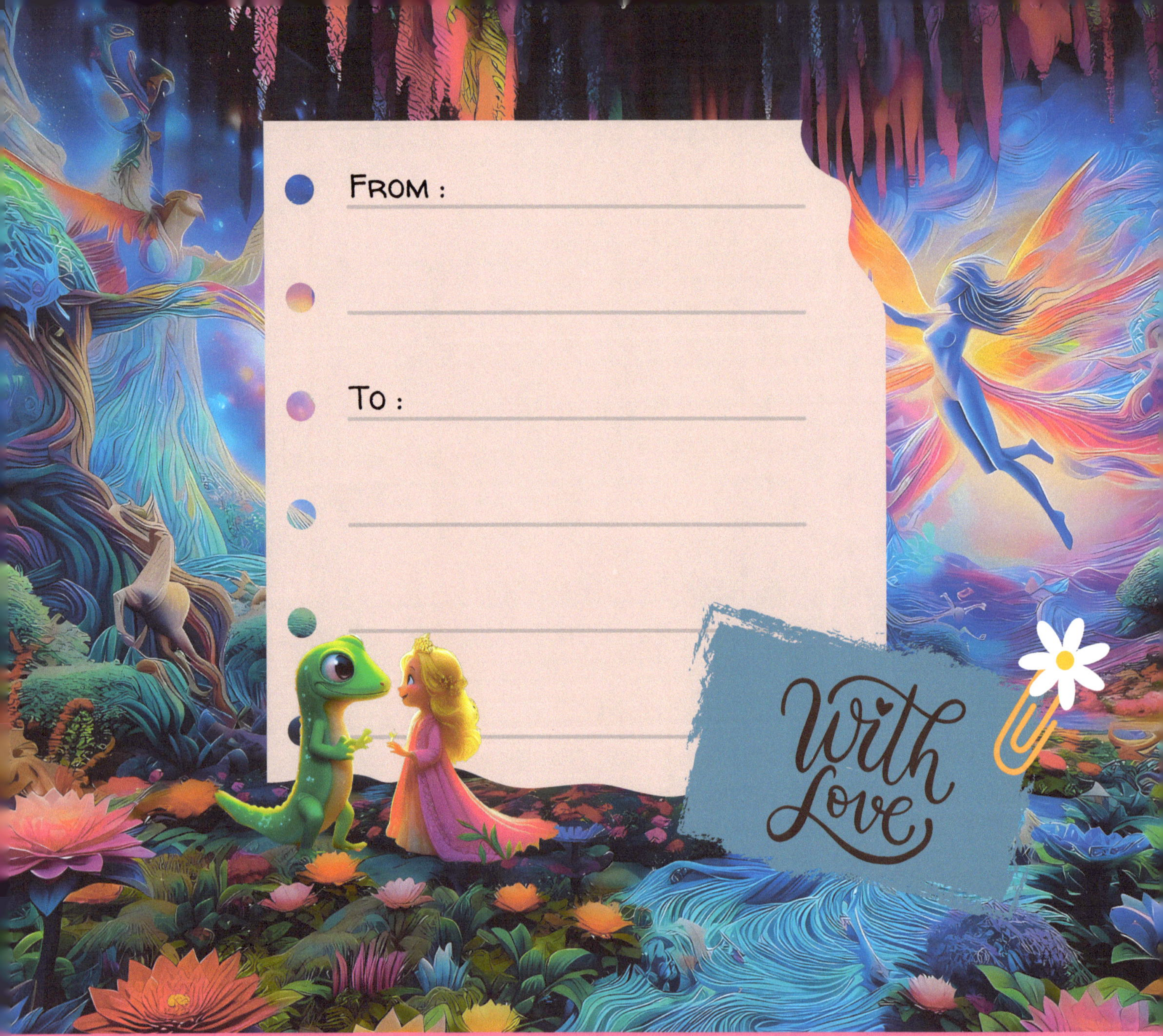

FROM :

____

____

TO :

____

____

____

With Love

Thank you for your purchase!
If you and your child enjoyed this book, a quick review
would mean the world to us. It takes just 5 seconds and
greatly supports small businesses like ours.

www.ingramcontent.com/pod-product-compliance
Lightning Source LLC
Chambersburg PA
CBHW042119110726
48006CB00002B/689